EFFECTIVE GOVERNANCE FOR THE TWENTY-FIRST CENTURY

BY

TONY MANERA

TABLE OF CONTENTS

INTRODUCTION

There are many good books available that cover the "nuts and bolts" of governance. What makes this work unique are its conciseness and in-depth coverage of performance measures. The conciseness should appeal to busy people who do not have the time nor the need to read lengthy academic texts. The emphasis on performance measures provides directors and management with important tools to establish and maintain a process of continuous performance improvement. A full chapter is entirely dedicated to this topic.

Effective governance in the twenty-first century is more demanding and more important than ever before. That is because the world has become more complex, with greater risks and more opportunities. Globalization affects all aspects of human activity. From the economy, to the environment to national and personal security, everything is connected to everything else. This reality has implications for how we govern different kinds of enterprises, whether they are in the public or private sector, for profit or non-profit.

The responsibility of ensuring effective governance belongs to the board of directors (The term "board of directors" is used

throughout this book to maintain
a consistent terminology.
Different organizations may use
other terms, such as "board of
trustees", "board of governors",
"governing council", etc.)

Good governance practices
alone cannot guarantee success;
sometimes an organization can be
quite effective despite poor
governance. That's because there
are many other important factors
at play. My point, however, is
that all other factors being
equal, the quality of governance
can make an important difference.
In other words, governance
matters.

I hope that after reading this
book, you will become a more
effective director. My thoughts

are also aimed at chief executive
officers and other senior
managers who regularly interact
with a board. I draw on my
service, over a period of about
thirty years, as a director on
non-profit and for profit boards,
as well as a CEO and senior
executive of medium and large
post-secondary educational and
broadcasting corporations. These
experiences have enabled me to
observe the interaction between
boards and senior management,
leading me to the conclusion that
it is essential for both groups
to have a proper understanding
and respect for each other's role
and responsibilities.

There are, of course, many
different types of boards. And

while some fundamental principles generally apply, methods of operation will necessarily vary. For example, the board of a large, for profit corporation whose shares trade on a public stock exchange will have to operate in an environment quite unlike that of a non-profit hospital board. Hence, my objective is not to suggest rigid rules that must always be followed, but rather to present a set of "best practices", subject to adaptation to specific circumstances.

The role of boards has come under increasing scrutiny in recent years. Many of us have read "horror stories" involving incompetence, fraud and corruption that have causedconsiderable financial losses to shareholders, employees, pensioners and taxpayers. This has happened despite the presumed effective scrutiny of these organizations by their own boards, government agencies, external auditors, analysts and so on. When evidence of management impropriety finally surfaces, we can all be justified in asking the question: "Where was the board?" In other words, had the board been sufficiently alert, and doing its job effectively, these disasters might have been avoided.

Governments and regulatory agencies have responded with

stronger legislation and regulations, which place greater

weight on boards by demanding that they discharge their fiduciary responsibilities much more effectively than has been the case in the past. In some cases, individual directors may be subject to heavy fines and even prison sentences if it can be demonstrated that they failed to act in accordance with the legal requirements that apply in their specific situation. Failure to ensure that appropriate safety and environmental protection standards are in place are examples of situations that can trigger serious legal consequences. Insider trading and other practices that enable directors and senior managers to profit from their privileged position fall in the same

category. A code of ethical business conduct, developed with appropriate legal advice, should be enshrined in the company's by-laws and made public.

In the U.S.A., a federal law, commonly referred to as "Sarbanes-Oxley Act of 2002", was passed in response to several accounting and corporate scandals at public companies such as Enron and WorldCom. Investors lost billions of dollars. The intent of this legislation is to protect investors by improving the accuracy and reliability of corporate disclosures. Other

countries have adopted similar
measures.

Among other measures,
Sarbanes-Oxley requires top
management of public companies to
certify that financial
information is accurate. Serious
penalties can result in cases of
fraud. Boards must comply with a
number of requirements related to
their oversight responsibilities.
This legislation also created a
"Public Company Accounting
Oversight Board", to ensure that
auditors are truly independent
and that there are appropriate
internal controls.

All boards should have
appropriate liability insurance
protecting their directors and

senior officers against civil lawsuits, but such insurance may have significant limitations and certainly will not shield a

person from prosecution and major financial and criminal penalties where laws have been broken.

In conclusion, while serving on a board carries significant responsibilities, it can also be very rewarding. The rewards may be financial (in the for profit sector) or non-financial (in the non-profit sector). In the latter case, you may derive considerable satisfaction from serving your community. In all cases, your life should be enriched by getting to know some interesting and dedicated people, and derive the benefits of the

intellectual stimulation that
comes from serving on a board of
directors.

BEFORE ACCEPTING A BOARD APPOINTMENT

It is most advisable that you perform "due diligence" before accepting an appointment as a member of a board of directors. You should know what you are getting yourself into before saying yes, even though you may be quite flattered in being invited to serve on a prestigious board. You should know why you are being asked to serve and what is expected of you. Is it because you have specialized knowledge and/or important contacts that can be of value to the organization? You should also know the time commitment that may be involved and the legal responsibilities that flow from board membership. You should ask yourself whether you may have a conflict of interest as a result of your involvement with other organizations. Finally, you should feel confident that you can make a worthwhile contribution to the objects of the organization on whose board you are considering to serve.

Several years ago I was invited to become a member of the board of a for profit corporation. I had specialized knowledge and many useful contacts in the business that this organization was planning to develop. The company was not yet operational, but had raised substantial quantities of venture capital to finance its initial operations, expecting to make a profit somewhere down the line. It had filed, as required by law, an extensive prospectus that described in detail the business plan, risks to be expected and a variety of other pertinent information that an investor would normally want to have. I had read the prospectus and found it quite thorough and well thought out.

My first board meeting was largely devoted to organizational matters. It was attended by legal counsel to ensure that certain resolutions that we were expected to adopt were properly documented. There were the usual

declarations that one has to make
regarding conflict of interest
and so on. Nothing particularly
unusual, except for a gut feeling
I developed during that first
meeting that I couldn't explain.
That feeling told me to be
careful. That's all.

The next day I found out what
my instincts were trying to tell
me. On my fax machine was a
formal notice from the Ontario
Securities Commission advising me
and all other directors that the
prospectus issued by the company
to raise venture capital had
failed to disclose important
material information. As a
director, I could be held civilly
and criminally responsible for
this act of omission. That got my

attention. Civil litigation was bad enough, but criminal prosecution for something that I had absolutely nothing to do with was even worse. I immediately resigned from this board and advised the Ontario Securities Commission of my decision, pointing out that I had not been on the board when the prospectus had been issued and, although I had read it, I could not be expected to have any knowledge of material omissions. Soon after, I spoke with the Commission's investigator and agreed to cooperate fully with their investigation. I had been on that board for only one day! Had I not resigned, I could have incurred significant financial costs for legal counsel, not to

mention the possibility of
prosecution. Luckily, the
investigator quickly realized
that I had not been a party to
any of the matters under
investigation and I was assured
that I was no longer a "person of
interest" in the matter.

The experience that I have
just described is not intended to
discourage anyone from serving on
a board. Society needs capable,
honest and dedicated individuals
who are prepared to perform
important duties on behalf of the
shareholders whose interests a
board is expected to protect and
to advance. It is simply a way
for me to illustrate the
importance of doing your homework
before accepting a board

appointment, and of course, throughout your term on the board of the organization with which you may become associated.

There are many ways to ensure that serving on a particular board will be a positive experience for yourself and the board. Most organizations now have websites that provide a wealth of information, including their governance policies and annual reports. An Internet search can uncover additional information that may not be widely known, but that you may find particularly useful. Speaking with current or past board members, the CEO or other persons familiar with the organization, when feasible, is another excellent way to obtain more pertinent insight. The process being used to recruit you can also be informative. Are there serious financial or personnel problems that you should be aware of? Aside from the general expectations that apply to every board member, are there specific expectations from you? And if so, are you comfortable with them?

If this is a non-profit company, are board members expected to be active in fund raising? Large non-profits generally have a separate foundation responsible for fund raising, but smaller entities expect their boards to participate in fund raising activities. Not everyone is suited to such a role. Some people are very good at it; others find it awkward. Be sure to find out before you accept a nomination to such a board.

Finally, no matter how well you do your homework, be prepared for possible surprises. These can occur not necessarily because anyone tried to hide something from you, but because of changes over which the company has no control, or sudden developments in the operating environment that could not be foreseen. Due diligence is a necessary, but not sufficient condition for success. This is true not only in governance matters, but for life in general. So assess the level

of risk and, if you are
comfortable, go for it!

THE ROLE OF A BOARD OF DIRECTORS

Every organization has, or ought to have, a purpose. The purpose is established by the shareholders. In the case of public service entities, such as publicly funded educational institutions, the purpose is established by the appropriate legislative bodies, to serve the public, who are the ultimate shareholders.

Unless it is very small and run by the shareholders themselves or by a group of volunteers, every organization employs people to manage and to

carry out its various functions.
These people, assuming that they
are competent and honest,
understand the business they are
in, and could, in many cases,
operate quite satisfactorily on
their own. In fact, I have known
many CEO's and senior managers
who considered their board to be
little more than a nuisance,
getting in their way, and making
their jobs more difficult than
they already were. They put up
with boards because they had to,
but manipulated them into rubber
stamping whatever management
wanted to do. This is
unfortunate, because it shows a
lack of recognition of the
respective roles of management
and board, but it does happen
from time to time. Of course,

there are also boards that insist on getting involved in day to day decisions that ought to be left to management. This is just as bad, and can lead to frustration and poorer results. So, apart from the need to satisfy certain legal requirements, why do we have boards?

The usual answer to this fundamental question is that we have boards to protect and to advance the shareholders' interests. Boards, after all, are usually elected or appointed by shareholders or legal representatives of shareholders. Boards perform their job by overseeing management; adopting the broad strategies necessary to realize the organization's goals;

selecting, evaluating, and when necessary, terminating senior officers;   monitoring the organization's performance; and approving certain major decisions recommended by management.

   The dividing line between board and management roles is not always clear cut. It can vary for all kinds of valid reasons. The size and complexity of the organization, the expertise of individual managers, directors and shareholders, the specific challenges and strategies being pursued, unusual problems that have developed, legal issues and a host of other factors can influence the actual division of labor between board and

management. There is simply no
single formula that can be used
to define the specific roles of
board and management at all
times. For this reason, I prefer
to differentiate board and
management roles by the
perspective that each brings to
their work. Boards must bring an
external perspective to their
oversight role. Management, no
matter how competent and
visionary, has a tendency to see
things from the inside. An
external perspective, when a
board does its job well, helps
management to see things as they
are perceived from the outside.
This interaction facilitates the
alignment of the interests of
management with the interests of

shareholders.

All organizations, if left to
their own devices, will pursue
their self interest. This may
not be in the best interests of
their shareholders. Equally
important, though more difficult
to define, it may not be in the
public interest. Governments are
notorious for establishing
commissions, agencies and other
entities to meet a legitimate
public purpose, but failing to
eliminate or change them when the
original need has ceased to exist
or changed in a significant way,
usually due to political
considerations.

The view that boards should
provide an external perspective

naturally raises the question of board composition, an important issue that will be addressed later on.

   For some time now, boards are also increasingly expected to take into account the interests of "stakeholders". Stakeholders may be employees, customers, taxpayers, communities affected by the company`s activities, and so on. More and more organizations are recognizing that taking into account stakeholders' interests is in their own long term interest. Annual reports and other public relations activities place increasing emphasis on being a responsible employer, protecting the environment, and generally contributing to the well-being of the communities in which they operate. Of course, unethical practices do occur, but the public is better informed than ever, and more active in challenging such behavior. Pension funds have become important players, due to their large holdings of shares in public companies, and they are using their clout to push for better governance practices. This is a good thing, and it influences in a significant way how boards discharge their responsibilities, not only to their shareholders, but also to the broader group of "stakeholders".

while providing an external

perspective is a valuable function of boards, there are considerable differences in how boards go about their business, just as there are considerable differences in how different organizations are managed. The often stated principle that boards make policy, while management implements it, is not very satisfying.

The fundamental problem with a definition of the board's role as policy maker is that what is policy can be far from clear. Some companies have thousands of written "policies", neatly organized in large binders, that provide instructions to employees on how to conduct the organization's business. Clearly

no board should get involved in
the development or approval of
such a large number of
"policies". If it did,
individual directors' jobs would
become full time, and represent a
waste of valuable talent. So, a
lot depends on how "policies" are
defined. One very successful
organization is reputed to have
only one policy. It instructs
all employees to do, at all
times, whatever they feel will
best advance the company's long
term interests. I doubt that
many organizations could function
in to-day's highly regulated
environment on the basis of such
a limited statement of policy,
but I am also convinced that the
performance of many organizations
could be substantially enhanced

by having fewer hard policies or rules and by placing greater authority, and responsibility in the hands of individual employees.

In fact, there is clearly a hierarchy of "policies". Strategic policies can be defined as those that describe the end results that an organization is pursuing. Such strategic policies are quite appropriate subjects for a board of directors to consider. But it does require that "end results" be identified and articulated.

Identifying desired end results is not always easy. In some cases, it may even be impossible. But the process of

trying to identify such results
can be quite beneficial, and
assist board and management to
focus their energies on what
really matters. Of course, it is
not sufficient to identify end
results, leaving all decisions on
means to achieve those end
results to the discretion of
management. Boards must also
establish boundaries on the scope
of management decisions.

Many boards adopt mission
statements, visions and values
that attempt to convey a sense of
what the company is trying to
achieve. These can be useful,
but due to their generally
abstract nature, do not merit too
great an investment of time. The
identification of desired end

results, which flows from the overall purpose of an organization, is a far more useful process in which a board of directors should be engaged.

The role of a board may therefore be summarized as follows:

1. Adoption of an overall strategy and goals (desired end results).
2. Anticipation of major risks and opportunities to ensure that the organization is well positioned to deal with them.
3. Development and implementation of an appropriate oversight

process; this should
include having by-laws
and policies in place
that provide guidance
to the CEO and other
employees in how the
company's business is
conducted.

4. Hiring, evaluating the
performance, setting
the compensation and,
if necessary, replacing
the CEO. Having a
succession plan for the
CEO and senior
management.

5. Ensuring that
appropriate performance
measures are
established and used in
a process of continuous
quality improvement.

BOARD COMPOSITION AND STRUCTURE

Board composition is generally prescribed in the board by-laws. These will have been set by the shareholders or their representatives. In the case of publicly funded agencies, the appropriate level of government will be responsible either for the actual appointment or the process to be followed to appoint board members. If a board has some power to select or influence the selection process, it should take full advantage of this opportunity to ensure that its

membership includes an
appropriate mix of people with
the skills and knowledge that
will be most helpful to the
organization. There should also
be an evaluation, professional
development and succession
mechanism in place for directors.

To add real value to an
organization, its board should be
made up of individuals with a
diverse range of skills and
knowledge. Diversity, when
properly implemented, will ensure
that a variety of perspectives
are brought to bear on the
board's deliberations. Those
perspectives would have been
shaped by each individual's
experience, knowledge and
judgment. Unfortunately, in

recent times, the concept of
diversity has been compromised by
a focus on representation by
gender, race and other factors.
There may be good public
relations considerations that
lead a board to adopt quotas for
visible minorities or other
categories of people. This well
meaning approach, however, is not
what I mean by diversity. As an
example, I once served on a board
where two-thirds of its members
were lawyers. They were all
capable individuals, but a better
mix would have included
engineers, economists, health
care practitioners, business
leaders, etc.

Many boards have term limits
for their members. This practice

has advantages and disadvantages.
The advantage is that fresh
thinking can be beneficial to the
work of the board, as different
people bring in new perspectives.
It also avoids awkward
situations where a long serving
member has outlived her/his
value. Term limits allow for a
graceful exit, without generating
bad feelings. On the other hand,
there is the risk of losing
exceptionally valuable talent,
when a member can no longer serve
on a board because he/she has
reached the maximum time period
allowed by the board's by-laws. A
similar conundrum arises with age
limits. There are clearly
arguments on both sides of the
question. Unless there are legal
requirements to the contrary, I

would opt for no term limits. In other words, while board members would be appointed for a specified term of so many years, there should be no prohibition to their re-appointment for additional terms, provided there is a credible evaluation process. The experience and knowledge gathered over a long period can be of great value to an organization. There is no guarantee that a new member will make a more valuable contribution to the work of the board than the member being replaced. Directors who are not chosen for re-appointment might experience hurt feelings, but this factor should not take precedence over the duty of a board to do whatever is in the best interests of its shareholders.

One note of caution is now in order. Depending on the nature of the organization, the CEO may have some influence in the selection of new directors. This is not necessarily a bad thing. After all, the CEO is bound to know many persons with the knowledge and skills that would be useful to the board. But there is also the danger that directors appointed through a recommendation or selection by the CEO will feel some sense of obligation that may very well cloud their judgment at critical junctures.

I used to be against having insiders, other than the CEO, as

members of a board of directors.
This view naturally flowed from
my belief that one of the most
fundamental roles of a board is
to provide an external
perspective. Having insiders on
a board could dilute the external
perspective and hence reduce the
overall effectiveness of a board.
I have changed my opinion on this
issue after having served on a
few boards with insider
participation. One was the board
of governors of Algonquin College
(a large community college in
Ottawa, Canada) and the other was
the Ottawa Hospital (a large
acute care hospital with a
significant academic and research
function). It was while serving
on these boards that I came to
realize and appreciate the "value

added" by the insiders' knowledge of the organization. Although the CEO is properly expected to know the organization he/she leads well enough to advise the board, that is not always the case, particularly in large and complex organizations. Having a few key insiders on a board can add very valuable insight. But there are some caveats to my support of insider membership on a board of directors.

The first caveat has to do with the ratio of insiders to outsiders. Insiders should never exceed 25% of a board's overall membership. This is arbitrary, as there is no perfectly objective way to establish the proper ratio. It's a judgment

call, based on the principle that
the dominant "drivers" of a board
should be outsiders. If a
company's shares trade on a stock
exchange, there will be
additional specific requirements
about the percentage of directors
who must qualify as
"independents." The company's by-
laws should explicitly outline
the standards that must be met by
a director to be considered
"independent", in accordance with
the applicable legal provisions.

The second caveat has to do
with the role that insiders see
themselves playing, and also how
the rest of the board perceives
their role. Sooner or later,
there will be a conflict of
interest. This applies not only

to insiders, but also to
outsiders. If insiders see
themselves or are seen by others
as "representing" the interests
of a particular group, then there
is greater potential for
conflicts of interest to arise.

Certain boards are
specifically established to
ensure that the interests of a
particular group are properly
advanced. A pension board, for
example, may have retirees and
employees on the board with a
specific expectation that they
are there to speak on behalf of
their constituencies. In such
cases, of course, the role of
these individuals is clearly
understood and quite properly
accepted. But, as a general

rule, individual board members, whether insiders or outsiders, should not be on the board to represent the interests of any specific group or organization to which they belong, but to advance the best interests of all shareholders on whose behalf they serve.

The bottom line is that insiders serving on a board can add value to the work of a board, provided that certain safeguards are adopted, ideally spelled out in the board's by-laws.

Another issue that arises in any examination of a board's role is whether the role of board chair and CEO should be combined or separated. Many highly successful organizations have the same person fill both roles. This may be due to the fact that the person in question is extremely capable, enjoys the full confidence of the board and the various shareholders, or it may simply be the way things have always been done in that particular organization. On the other hand, where the same person occupies both roles, it makes it more difficult for the board to fully reflect an outsider's perspective. This exposes the board and the company to more risk. Too much power in the hands of one person may not cause any problem for a while, but it is not in the best long term interests of the organization. Therefore, unless there are

compelling reasons to merge the
two positions, it is better that
the position of board chair be
filled by a different person than
the CEO.

I speak from experience in
this regard. For a while during
my time as president and CEO of
the Canadian Broadcasting
Corporation, the position of
board chair became vacant. The
legal framework under which this
crown corporation operated,
provided that if the position of
chair was vacant, the president
would be acting as chair. I found
this arrangement uncomfortable
and would have preferred for the
board to select one of its
external members as chair, but
this was not legally possible.

Of course, separating the two
roles has its own set of risks.
The CEO and chair may not get
along. They may have different
visions of where the organization
should be going or how it should
pursue its broad strategy.
Whether it's a personality
conflict or simply a different
way of seeing things, conflict
between the individuals who
occupy these positions can cause
serious problems. It can be
particularly difficult when both
individuals have strong
personalities and are unable to
resolve their differences. The
situation can be made worse when
the role of each person is not
spelled out or is somewhat vague.
In the end, it's up to each board
to decide how it wants to resolve

this question should it arise. The important thing is not to allow it to fester. The same rule applies to conflict among other directors. Some differences of opinion are to be expected and can, in fact, serve a constructive purpose. But if the conflict is substantive and ongoing, the board chair should take the leadership role in resolving it as soon as possible. Outside assistance in conflict resolution may be required in some cases.

My point, therefore, is not to advance any specific governance model, but to suggest that some attention be given to the respective roles of board chair and CEO, and whether the roles should be separate or combined. And while I obviously believe that the separation of roles is usually the best long term solution, I also have to acknowledge that this is not a science, and that combining the two roles may work very well in some cases.

Another important issue is that of board committees. Some boards have no committees at all, others have too many. There is no hard and fast rule that tells us which committee structure is best for a particular organization, but some general principles can be applied.

If a board is relatively small (I have served on boards with as

few as five members) then
committees are not necessary.
From a practical standpoint,
there are simply not enough
members to go around. Quorums
become an issue, as the absence
of a single board member can
result in a lack of quorum.

Most boards, however, have
from nine to twenty board
members. Now a committee
structure can make sense. The
following list is not meant as a
rigid prescription of what
committees a board should have. I
offer it only as a starting point
for discussion and decision by
each board.

Sometimes issues discussed in
a committee get rehashed at a

full board meeting. Some of this is probably unavoidable, but generally, committees should be where directors can examine in more detail important issues that fall within their mandate. Committees can also operate more informally than a full board, and allow input by knowledgeable individuals who are not board members. Each committee chair should then report to the full board. Unless an issue is particularly important, or contentious, the board shouldn't spend a lot of time debating it if it has already been addressed at the committee level. I know that there is a danger of the board becoming a rubber stamping body, with key decisions effectively made by a smaller group of directors who happen to serve on a committee. This is where a good board chair can judge whether an issue that has been dealt with at a committee level also requires thorough discussion by the full board. It is really a judgement call. Obviously, if every issue that has received close scrutiny by a committee is debated at length by the board, then one has to question whether that particular committee adds any value to the work of the board of directors.

FINANCE

This is probably the most common board committee. It is the

committee that should be
responsible for the examination

of budget and major spending
proposals, making appropriate
recommendations to the full
board. It is also where regular
financial reports are examined at
monthly or quarterly intervals.

OPERATIONS

There should be some committee
that oversees the company's
operations. This does not mean
that directors should get
involved in day to day management
decisions. They should, however,
have a process in place that

provides them with regular
reports on the performance of the
organization. Here is where

directors can and should ask a
lot of questions, so that the
board can effectively discharge
its oversight responsibilities.

HUMAN RESOURCES

A human resources committee
will concern itself with how
effectively the company manages
its "most important asset", as
most organizations like to
characterize their human
resources. In unionized
workplaces, the board needs to
know and approve the collective

bargaining strategies recommended by management. There are issues of compensation, working conditions, succession, evaluation, etc. that will benefit from the deliberations of such a committee.

AUDIT

It is essential to have an audit committee, preferably chaired by an outside director who is knowledgeable about audit issues. The Audit Committee should be separate from the Finance Committee. The CEO should be present for each meeting of this committee, but should not exercise a vote. External

auditors should be retained by
the board upon recommendation by
the audit committee. Care must be
taken to ensure that the auditing
firm does not have a conflict of
interest. Such a conflict could
arise if the same auditors are
retained to do other work for the
company. Some organizations also
have an internal auditor who
complements the work of external
auditors. The internal auditor
should be independent of the
finance department. It is not a
bad idea to change external
auditors every few years. Even
when the same auditing firm is
used, there is merit in rotating
individual auditors.

EXECUTIVE

Generally, a board's executive committee is made up of the chairs of all standing committees, as well as the board chair. It can serve various purposes. One of them is to set the board's agenda, as well as the terms of reference or mandates of individual committees. Individual board members, however, should be able to suggest specific agenda items for discussion by the board. The Executive Committee is also a good place to develop or review the board's by-laws, recruit new board members, receive performance reports of senior management from the CEO, evaluate

the CEO's performance, set the
CEO's compensation package,
ensure a proper succession plan,
establish ad hoc committees as
needed, nominate candidates to
serve as committee members and
chairs as well as board chair and
vice-chair, and when necessary,
to set up a search committee to
find the next CEO. There could
very well be additional duties
that the executive committee can
perform, however, care must be
taken not to allow it to be seen
to usurp the role of the full
board of directors. It is very
easy to create the impression
that there is an "inner group"
that makes all the important
decisions. The executive
committee chair could be simply
the board's vice-chair, who would

act as chair in the event that
the regular board chair is
unavailable.

AD HOC

From time to time, issues
arise that don't quite fit the
mandate of existing (standing)
committees. The board of
directors should consider
establishing an "ad hoc"
committee with a specific task.
Once the ad hoc committee has
reported its findings and
recommendations to the board, it
is dissolved. Depending on the
issue, such committees can
benefit from external expert
input. The composition should

reflect individual directors' area of expertise as well as desire to become involved.

ROTATION OF DIRECTORS

There is merit in rotating directors among different committees, provided this does not deprive the board of access to specialized knowledge (audit or finance, for example) of value to a specific committee. Rotating membership enables directors to acquire a more complete understanding of the company's challenges and hence are better able to see the big picture than if they are confined to a single committee.

STRATEGY

I have not suggested a committee that would deal with strategy. I feel that all members of a board of directors should participate in any discussion of strategy.

One of the tools that every board should have (to be included in its by-laws) is the capacity to meet by teleconference when matters of urgency must be dealt with.

Given the foregoing, the reader should by now have realized how important is the role of chair, whether of the full board or of committees. A good chair will provide ample

opportunities for individual
directors to ask questions or
express opinions, and will know
when the time is right to put
whatever issue is being debated
to a formal vote. Not everyone is
suited to chair board meetings.
One of the techniques that is
often used by boards is to have a
brief (five minute max)
evaluation of each meeting after
it ends. It gives directors an
opportunity to vent while the
proceedings are still fresh. For
example, if an individual
director feels that an item was
not sufficiently debated, that
point can be made. One may also
raise questions as to whether an
item really was important enough
to be included on the agenda.
These and other points should

enable the chair to obtain a
clearer sense of how the members
perceived the effectiveness of
the meeting.

Chairs of a board or one of
its committees should be
sensitive to the views of their
members, but not to the point
where their hands are too tightly
bound. Individual members should
also recognize some warning signs
that all is not well. One of them
is meetings that drag on and on,
aimlessly, without a clear focus
on what the meeting is supposed
to achieve. The role of chair is
to communicate clearly what the
object of any particular
deliberation is, and steer the
discussion towards a proper
disposition of the item in

question. Another is having too
few or too many meetings. Of
course, this is subjective and
there may very well be valid
reasons for infrequent or
frequent meetings. If the reasons
are known, then there is no
problem. But, if they aren't,
then that should raise a flag.

Another warning sign to watch
out for is the receipt of
documents at the last minute.
Normally, documents should be
circulated several days before a
meeting takes place. Occasionally
there may be valid reasons why a
document could not be prepared in
advance. But, if this happens too
often, then directors should be
concerned. Here again, what is
"too often" is a judgment call.

But that is what directors are expected to do: use their best judgment!

Ideally, management should ensure that there are "no surprises" for board members. Nothing upsets directors more than reading in a newspaper or seeing on television something about the organization that they are supposed to govern, yet were not aware of. To be fair, management cannot control what the press will report. And hence, a distinction must be made between reports that could not be reasonably anticipated and those that could and should have been seen coming. Too many surprises and the board needs to take a long hard look at how the company is being managed.

As a general rule, the CEO (or delegate) is the official spokesperson for the company. Individual directors should never speak publicly on any issue related to their board responsibilities. This is very important for several reasons. The first, of course, is to ensure consistency of message. If there is any real or perceived difference among directors, the media will pick it up and that can cause real problems. The other has to do with the skill set necessary to communicate with the media. Not everyone is a good communicator and some people can easily get caught up in perceived inconsistencies or contradictions. Presumably the CEO (or delegate) knows how to communicate; if not, then the board has a problem.

There are, of course, instances when it is more appropriate for the board chair (or someone designated by the board chair) to speak publicly on behalf of the company. An obvious example is if the CEO has been or will be replaced. Or it may be necessary for the board to publicly indicate its confidence in the CEO when necessary but unpopular decisions have been made. There may be other instances when such a departure from normal protocol is warranted. This should be the subject of discussion between the

CEO and chair, to ensure that
both are operating on the same
wavelength. Real damage can be
inflicted when the board and CEO
do not appear to be "singing from
the same hymn book!"

CONFLICT OF INTEREST

It may be useful at this point to briefly address the concept of conflict of interest. Anybody who serves on a board, whether as an insider or as an outsider, may at some point encounter a conflict of interest. There is nothing wrong with having a conflict of interest; what counts is how it is handled. If the conflict is frequent, or ongoing, then of course such an individual should either not serve on the board, or terminate the activity that gives rise to the conflict. For example, if you serve on several boards, your fiduciary role as a member of one board can put you in conflict with your role as a member of another board, in which case you should choose which board you want to be associated with and resign from the other board. If there is a change in your position or other external responsibilities, you should ascertain whether the change creates a conflict of interest.

Where the conflict is infrequent, there is no reason why an individual should not serve on a board.   All boards should have in their by-laws a set of rules for dealing with conflicts of interest. These rules will naturally vary, and should reflect the specific needs

74

of the organization. But one
fundamental principle always
applies. And that principle is
"disclosure". If you think you
have a conflict of interest, or
could be perceived to have a
conflict of interest, then you
must disclose the nature of the
conflict. Disclosure resolves
the vast majority of conflicts.
Furthermore, where a genuine
conflict exists, the individual
should not participate in any
discussion or decision that could
be influenced by the conflict. It
is also important to keep in mind
that "perceptions" of a conflict
of interest can be as important
as actual conflicts.

STRATEGY

"Our long term strategy is to survive and do nothing stupid; our short term strategy is to get to the long term strategy"

Author Unknown

Notwithstanding the humorous quote above, strategy is key to the success or failure of any organization. It should bring together the broad elements necessary to achieve certain desired end results. A board of directors should play a key role in the establishment of an organization's strategy, in conjunction with the CEO. The CEO, in fact, should provide the leadership necessary to formulate strategy. The exact process will vary from one organization to another, but some ideas worthy of consideration are offered below.

It may be useful to distinguish short term strategy from long term strategy. The former can be more precisely defined, but it should link up with the latter. Obviously, the further one looks into the future, the greater the uncertainty. A process that I have found useful is for a board of directors to have an annual retreat during which its members engage in a "brainstorming" process. The object is to generate a set of about a dozen key strategic goals that can then be refined and analyzed before final adoption at a subsequent meeting. The CEO, several senior managers and sometimes one or more knowledgeable outsiders should participate as equals. This will only work if the CEO and the board have developed the kind of trusting relationship that makes it possible for individuals to freely express their opinion. A retreat along the lines described above can also serve the very useful function of team building and professional development for both board members and the management group. Considerable work ahead

of such a retreat is normally
required. There may be reading
material to be circulated,
position papers prepared, outside
experts identified and so on. And
while it's important to have a
relatively informal process, care
must be taken to remain focussed
on the desired end result. Too
much informality will have people
rambling in too many directions.
Too rigid a process will
discourage creativity and
spontaneity. An experienced
facilitator should be retained to
ensure that the right balance is
maintained.

   Any discussion of strategy
should begin with an
environmental assessment. By this
I mean understanding where the

organization is at the moment
when compared to similar
organizations. More importantly,
where is the organization headed
if it continues along on its
current path? You can't develop
an appropriate strategy for the
future if you don't know or fully
understand the company's current
state.

An important element in the
development of an effective
strategy is the identification of
risks and opportunities. This is
where a properly constituted
board of directors can make a
real and positive difference. Of
course, no one can predict the
future. But knowledgeable
individuals can anticipate events
that could affect the

organization on whose board they
serve. This can be done through
the type of brainstorming process
to which I have already referred.

Risks and opportunities can be
classified in terms of their
probability of occurrence as well
as the importance of their
impact. An earthquake may be a
low probability event, but carry
huge negative consequences. A
union strike may have a medium
probability with a range of
potential consequences. Because
of globalization, events in far
off lands can have almost
immediate impacts on local
operations. Similarly,
technological developments can
render current business models
obsolete very quickly. Risk

management has developed into a fairly important discipline. Directors should learn as much as possible about the latest techniques involved in assessing risk, but they should also focus on potential opportunities to advance their organization's goals. The object is not to eliminate all risk, as that is impossible, but to mitigate damage from predictable risks through the development of appropriate contingency plans. At the same time, the board and senior management should ensure that the company is well positioned to take advantage of new opportunities that may present themselves. Sometimes risks can be transformed into opportunities.

Another important board
responsibility is to know that a
company's assets are put to their
best possible use. Assets is a
rather broad term. It includes
physical plant and equipment,
intellectual property, human
resources, investments, cash,
other companies, brand etc.
Creating an inventory of all
classes of assets and determining
whether they are being deployed
in the best possible way can be a
stimulating and rewarding
exercise.

OVERSIGHT

A board's oversight role is extremely important. It flows from its fiduciary duty to ensure that the best interests of shareholders are always pursued.

How the board performs this role will vary from one organization to another. Management will bring reports, some in writing, others orally, before the board and/or one of its committees. Directors should carefully read or listen to such reports, in order to ask

questions and to be satisfied
that the company is well run.

Some directors are reluctant
to ask questions. They should get
over such reluctance. It is
better to ask too many questions
than too few. The board or
committee chair has an important
role to play in ensuring that
each director has ample
opportunities to ask questions
and also to disallow questions
that may be inappropriate for
valid reasons. Such discretion
should be used very sparingly.

It is important for the board
to make it clear that asking
questions is not the same as
questioning. A director may, for
example, ask why a particular

policy or practice exists. That should not be interpreted as questioning the validity or appropriateness of such a policy or practice. To the extent that it is seen as such, it will probably result in a defensive response by management. Management must realize that a large component of the job of directors is to ask questions. And directors, of course, should be careful not to imply wrongdoing by the way they choose to frame their questions (unless they really mean to, in which case the board as a whole needs to be seized of the issue).

The foregoing illustrates how important it is to have an open, respectful and honest

relationship between a board of
directors and its senior
management. This does not happen
by chance. Both parties must work
at it. If such a relationship
exists, then the potential for
misunderstandings, hurt feelings
and worse is minimized.

PERFORMANCE MEASURES

WHY MEASURE PERFORMANCE?

There are many good reasons
for measuring performance. I will
list five, all of which are aimed
at improving a company's
performance. These are:
*accountability, advocacy,
effective management, fulfilment
of a board's fiduciary duties* and
*setting the company's strategic
direction.*

Accountability to shareholders
is at the top of the list.

Whoever you are expected to represent, you have a duty of accountability to them. Performance measures are a tool that will assist you in the performance of your duties a board member.

Advocacy on behalf of the company on whose board you sit may also be quite important, either occasionally or on a continuous basis. You may not be the person who will actually perform the advocacy role, but whoever does will be better equipped if there are valid performance measures.

Advocacy is particularly important in the non-profit sector. Whether it's a government agency, or potential donors, or other interested parties, you can only go so far in influencing them with subjective arguments. At some point, you will need hard data, such as performance measures, to really make your case.

In the for profit sector, advocacy is no less important. Most organizations are affected by government policies, legislation and public opinion. They need to get their message out to some or all of these constituencies. That message will be more convincing if it is backed by appropriate performance measures.

Management and board members

need performance measures to ensure *effective management* of the organization. If you don't measure performance, how can you improve it? Managers will generally require a larger and more detailed set of performance measures than a board of directors. But all measures should be based on the same data elements. All players need performance measures as valuable tools for the continuous improvement of performance.

Fulfilment of a board's fiduciary duties requires directors to ask questions of management.   Armed with appropriate performance measures will make it possible for you to ask more relevant and important questions.

Finally, the process by which
directors and senior management
develop and use performance
measures can serve as a catalyst
for *setting the company's
strategic direction.*

WHAT ASPECTS OF PERFORMANCE

SHOULD BE MEASURED?

Performance measures should
be driven by the end results
that flow from an organization's
purpose. Management and board
should define desired end results
together. In fact, there should
be considerable interaction

between board and management in the process leading to the identification of performance measures linked to desired end results. For management to simply present a list of performance measures to the board for its approval misses the whole point of having a board in the first place. A passive board, which rubber stamps management's proposals is not doing its job. Equally unwise would be for a board establishing performance measures without management input. Best results are achieved through an iterative process where both management and board agree on the desired end results and consequential performance measures.

How end results are expressed
depends on the nature of the
organization. Some organizations
produce goods (automobiles,
computers, commodities, etc.)
Other organizations provide
services (health care, education,
engineering, etc.) In many
cases, both goods and services
are provided.

In the case of goods, end
results can usually be expressed
in numbers. You can produce so
many widgets per month, at a
certain cost, making a profit of
so many dollars, pounds, euros
or some other currency. This
translates into a quarterly or
annual profit, from which taxes
and dividends are paid. If the
company is public, its share

price on stock exchanges will also be numerically expressed.

In the case of services, end results can also be expressed numerically in a profit making company. In the non-profit sector, some end results can be expressed numerically, but this is not always the case. Deciding what should be measured, how it should be measured, and what importance should be attached to the results all involve judgment calls.

What all this adds up to is that boards and management should agree on what end results are desired, expressed numerically where this is possible, but also consider end results that defy

quantitative measurement, because
such results can also be
important. You can count how
many people buy a ticket to a
musical performance, and how much
profit or loss the performance
produces, and that may be all
that you are interested in
knowing, but there is an argument
to be made for also being
interested in the quality of that
performance. Of course, quality
is subjective. There is no
quality meter for every desirable
outcome, but that does not mean
that quality is not important. In
fact, sometimes things that
cannot be measured are more
important than things that can be
measured. In the words of Albert
Einstein: "*Not everything that
counts can be counted, and not*

everything that can be counted, counts."

Directors and senior management should, from time to time, review performance measures to ensure that they continue to be relevant and add value to the company's operations. It may be that certain performance measures fall in the category of "it's nice to know", but aren't sufficiently important to justify the time and cost involved in their production. A good test of the value of any such measure is whether anyone uses it and for what purpose. Resources required to collect and organize data that does not contribute to performance improvement represent an opportunity cost.

ATTRIBUTES OF A USEFUL

PERFORMANCE MEASUREMENT SYSTEM

Any system of performance measurement should satisfy five key criteria. These are: *importance, relevance, validity, limitations and consistency of methodology.*

The most obvious characteristic of any performance measure is its *importance*. If it is not sufficiently important, why waste time on it? Obviously, importance is sometimes subjective. That's why a healthy debate on the relative importance of a specific measure is valuable.

Closely related to importance is *relevance*. These two criteria aren't mutually exclusive. They should be looked at in the context of the intended user. If an automobile manufacturer experiences an increased demand for red cars and a reduced demand for black cars, management needs to know this, in order to have more red paint than black paint. Hence, the information is relevant for management. But the board of directors wouldn't normally be concerned with such a detail. In other words, this is not really an important performance measure for the board of directors. On the other hand, if demand for the company's four wheel drive vehicles increases, substantial capital investments may be required to switch assembly lines from two wheel drives to four wheel drives. In this case, the issue is important and relevant for both the board of directors and management.

Importance and relevance are necessary but not sufficient characteristics of an effective performance measuring system. *Validity* is also essential. As a society, we tend to attach more significance to information that has a number in front of it. Numbers imply, but do not necessarily guarantee, precision.

Every day newspapers carry stories with numbers in them.

Business stories, of course, tend
to focus on financial
information. Opinion polls
attempt to quantify public
opinion on some issue of public
interest. We are inundated with
numbers. Now, as an engineer, I
love numbers! But I also have a
healthy respect for the
limitations of numbers.   If one
takes the time to dig, and find
out how a particular number was
arrived at, one often discovers
that the number is far from
precise. Financial statements
and opinion polls, for example,
involve numbers. But such
numbers are often subject to
interpretation.

The most serious validity
issue with numbers is outright

fraud. It is possible to lie with numbers. It happens every day, and people sometimes go to jail for it.

To assess the validity of any performance measure expressed in numbers, one needs to understand not only what has been measured, but also how it was measured. Responsible opinion pollsters go to great lengths to explain the methodology used to conduct their polls. They will tell you the actual question that was asked, how they selected their sample, what the margin of error is, and so on. Poll results can be very misleading for all kinds of reasons, such as the sequence of questions that were asked, the way the sample was chosen, the timing of the question, and a host of other factors. Usually, we don't pay much attention to these things, even when the pollster has done a good job of pointing them out. We tend to see the headline, and even if we read the qualifications that are described in the full article, what tends to stick in our mind is the headline.

Board members must develop a basic understanding of the meaning and *limitations* of the various numbers that will be presented to them. Some very competent and valuable board members will not have the aptitude or interest to develop this understanding, but there should be a sufficient number of board members with the ability to interpret and judge the vast amount of numerical information that is available to them.

The most common numerical information that all boards will be asked to review is financial. Whether your company produces goods or services or both, and whether it's a for profit or non-profit entity, money will be raised and money will be spent. Financial information not only enables a board to judge the financial performance of the organization, but it can also provide very useful insight into other aspects of the operation. If you really want to understand what goes on inside an organization, a very good technique is to follow the money. It won't tell you everything, of course, but it will tell you a lot, and prompt you, if you are so inclined, to learn about things that you would never find out otherwise.

You don't need to be an accountant to understand financial statements. If you have experience at a senior management or board level, in all likelihood, you already know a lot about this. If you have no such experience, there are many good books that explain basic properties of financial statements, and it would be worth your while to read one of these books, especially those meant for the lay person, whose only interest in financial matters is to enable her/him to do a responsible job as a member of a board of directors.

Whichever group you belong to, there are a few pointers that you may find helpful. First of all, you need to remember that, in the preparation of financial statements, assumptions must be made. Assumptions are based on judgment calls. One example is the present day cost of future liabilities, such as pension and benefit costs. The apparent health of a pension fund will depend on what assumptions are made about inflation, rate of return on investments, life expectancy of pensioners, future size of workforce, etc. Even minor variations in one of these assumptions can have a significant impact on whether the fund is judged sufficient to meet its obligations.   There are also accounting rules, some established by the accounting profession, others by government regulations or by the company itself. For example, at what point is it appropriate to recognize revenue? Is it when a customer has placed the order, or is it when the product has been delivered? Or is it when the customer has actually paid for the product? It is very important for a board member to understand on what basis revenue is reported. Accounts receivable are another matter of interest. Someone must make an assumption as to what portion of accounts receivable can be realistically recognized as revenue, and what portion should be written off as uncollectible. The same applies to lawsuits. Large companies can have hundreds of lawsuits at any given time. Someone has to make a judgment call on the likely outcome of such lawsuits, and make appropriate provision in the company's finances. This is not a science, and honest and competent individuals can sometimes make some quite wrong assumptions. The greater the financial risk of any given assumption, the more closely should senior management and the board of directors examine such assumptions. As we all know from reading the business pages of our daily newspapers, financial reports can also be manipulated. Dishonest people can get away with such manipulation for years, and sometimes they are never caught.

One would think that that's what auditors should be looking at. And, of course, auditors do examine financial statements before they give their opinion. But lately, auditors have become very cautious and tend to produce opinions so full of caveats that it makes you wonder just how much reliance a board or shareholder can place on an audit report. Quite often, for example, auditors will say in their letter certifying a company's financial performance, that they cannot

guarantee that fraud has not or
is not occurring. Financial
statements are basically the
responsibility of management;
auditors only give an opinion
(hopefully a well informed
opinion) as to the fairness of
financial statements. Of course,
auditors provide a very valuable
service, and sometimes they can
smell something fishy and raise
flags. My point is that an audit
report, even a very thorough one,
does not and should not, reduce
management and board
responsibility to ask a lot of
questions, and ensure that they
fully understand what the
financial statements say, as well
as what they don't say. It is
particularly important that
directors read and fully

understand the various notes that
form an important part of
financial statements. Sometimes
the notes reveal a lot of
information that a board of
directors should further examine.

  What about performance
measures other than those found
in common financial statements?
These may or may not have a
bearing on the company's
finances, but they do provide a
tool to enable people to judge
how well a company is doing in a
number of areas. A useful
performance measure for an
automobile manufacturer, for
example, could be the percentage
of buyers who are satisfied with
their purchase six months or a
year after the purchase. I'm sure

automobile manufacturers would like this measure to be 100% at all times, but that is not likely to happen. The value of such a measure, in fact, may not lie in the number itself, but in the change from a previous period (is it getting better or worse?), or perhaps through a comparison with the results for a competing manufacturer.

Thus it is crucial when comparing performance measures, either with a prior period, or with those of another similar organization, to ensure *consistency of methodology* for collecting such information. There is no value in being told that this year 95% of our buyers were satisfied, whereas last

year, only 90% were satisfied if
the methodology for arriving at
this number changed along the
way. Other factors, outside
one's control, can also influence
a change in reported performance
measures. Understanding the
factors that are responsible for
a particular change can point to
areas that require improvement.
But if the numbers are not
sufficiently comparable,
decisions might be made on the
basis of apparent changes, not
real changes.

Governments provide a perfect
example of my point. We all know
that when the economy is doing
well, governments automatically
claim that this is the result of
their wise and sound policies.

When the economy does poorly, governments are quick to blame either previous governments, or forces outside their control. In fact, nothing is ever black and white. You can sometimes have a good economy in spite of lousy government policies. At other times, governments will have done all the right things, but the economy stinks. Economies, just like the weather, are too complex to establish a clear cause and effect relationship between any two variables. There are certainly situations where this is the case, but not always. The same is true of companies. Management generally takes credit for increases in profits, but finds all kind of explanations for reduced profits or losses, short of their own incompetence.

As a general rule, I have learned that no important judgments should be made on the basis of a single performance measure, because no single performance measure can capture all of the important end results that an organization is designed to achieve. You really need to look at several, each focusing on a different aspect of a company's operations. Only when the full picture is seen and understood can good decisions be made. Also important is not to have too many performance measures. Being swamped by numbers makes it difficult to focus attention on what really matters. Decisions should be based on information,

not data. Information must be as
accurate as possible, it must be
relevant to the desired end
results, and above all, must be
fully understood, which also
requires a clear appreciation of
its limitations.

Whenever possible, information
provided by independent external
sources should be used to
complement or supplement
internally generated data.
External validation adds
credibility and leads to better
decisions in the long run.

To summarize this chapter, the
following points should be
emphasized:

Performance measures must be
important, relevant and valid.

Validation is enhanced when measures are externally generated or when the methodology used to produce them is independently verified.

No single performance measure is sufficient for a complete assessment of a company's performance. Several measures may be required, sometimes covering a period of time. Under such circumstances, care must be taken to ensure consistency of methodology.

Having too many metrics can be just as bad as having too few. It can be confusing and detract from a board's ability to focus on what is most in need of attention.

All performance measures have limitations that should be understood before decisions based on such measures are finalized.

BOARD – MANAGEMENT

RELATIONSHIP

The principal and most important board-management relationship is the one with the company's chief executive officer. The CEO is the board's chief adviser and the person on whom the board relies for leadership and execution of the company's business plan.

This does not preclude a board receiving information or advice from individuals other than the CEO. In many cases, members of senior management may very well make recommendations to a board or one of its committees, but this should normally take place only with the CEO's prior knowledge and consent. The same can be said about the board or one of its members seeking advice from external sources. The board must retain the right to seek such advice, especially on, but not limited to, legal and audit issues without having to go through management. Nevertheless, unless the board has lost confidence in the CEO, in which case other steps should be taken, it would be inadvisable for the CEO to be kept in the dark about such matters. It risks undermining the CEO's leadership and effectiveness.

On the other hand, directors should not hesitate to ask senior

management members routine
questions on readily available
information without having to go
through the CEO. This should be
done with some sensitivity, to
avoid creating the impression
that the board is by-passing the
CEO or placing senior managers in
an awkward position. If the
relationship between board, CEO
and senior management is one of
confidence, this should not be an
issue. Requests by the board for
information that requires
substantial investment of time,
however, should be channelled
through the CEO. A board should
never give instructions or
direction to any member of the
senior management team other than
the CEO.

Two other sources of advice to
which the board should have
direct access are legal and
audit. The board must always be
satisfied that it is operating
within the law and that financial
records are properly kept. Unless
there is a serious problem of
trust, in which case other steps,
to be described later, must be
taken, the CEO should be present
whenever such legal or audit
advice is being requested or
received by the board of
directors. There may be instances
when the CEO is not in agreement
with legal or audit advice being
provided to the board. This
should rarely happen, but there
could be legitimate reasons, of
which the board should be made
aware, for such disagreements.

Sometimes there are grey areas that call for judgement calls, and the board should keep an open mind. Legal advice, for example, may come in the form of: "On one hand......, on the other hand...", when the legality of a particular decision cannot be absolutely established, in which case, sound judgement should prevail.

Sooner or later, a board will have to appoint a new CEO. There may be a process already in place for making such a decision, or the board may have to develop one from scratch. A lot depends on the circumstances that have led to a vacancy. The CEO may simply have retired, or found another job, or the board has decided that new leadership is required.

It's up to the board to decide to what extent the departing CEO should be consulted about potential successors.

If the CEO is retiring, presumably the board has had some time to prepare for the succession. If one or more internal candidates have been identified as having the required leadership qualities, and the board is satisfied with the company's direction, then there may be no need for an external search. Appointing someone from within is usually a morale booster, and reflects well on the company's management and governance. It also signals a degree of continuity that may reassure investors and other stakeholders. Of course, if there are several internal candidates who see themselves worthy of consideration, those who are not selected may resent the choice. In some cases, they may even decide to leave the company. While the board should not be insensitive to these human considerations, it should not be unduly influenced by people's hurt feelings. Disappointments are part of the job for senior management. The good ones understand this and swallow their pride, waiting for another opportunity or accepting that they are not likely to get the top job. Those who can't live with the decision would be wise to plan for their own exit.

Even when there is one or more
internal candidates ready to
assume the CEO's mantle, the
board may find it desirable to
conduct a full search, including
both insiders and outsiders. This
is understandable. There may be a
more competent or visionary
leader outside the company and
the board should not be reluctant
to aim for the best. The only
caveat I would offer is that
there is no perfect candidate.
The board is likely to know the
weaknesses of internal candidates
(or can easily find out what they
are), while the weaknesses of
external candidates may not come
to light until after they have
been on the job for a while. This
can happen even after undertaking
the most thorough reference

checks.

Of course, the board could feel that a change in direction is called for and that internal candidates, even if they are very competent, are simply unable or unwilling to make the course adjustments that the board believes are needed. In this case, a CEO who is experienced at change management should be sought.

Whatever the board's rationale for carrying out a full search, it would be wise to establish a small ad hoc committee (or make use of an existing executive committee) for this purpose. Its mandate would be to oversee the search process and to make a

recommendation to the full board
in due course. Unless the
organization is relatively small,
and the directors can devote the
required time, an executive
search company should be
retained. Seeking candidates,
interviewing them and performing
background checks is time
consuming work. A firm that
specializes in executive search,
particularly if it has a good
track record in the relevant
field, can do most of the leg
work that is required to narrow
down the list of qualified
candidates for the board's
consideration. Such consultants
are expensive, but the good ones
are worth their fees. The board
may already know a reputable firm
or may seek proposals from

different firms. They all charge
pretty well the same, so the key
factor will not be cost, but
track record.

When the departure of the CEO
does not allow enough time for a
successor to take over, an
interim appointment must be made.
Unless there has been a problem,
the CEO should be able to make an
appropriate recommendation to the
board.

Whatever the circumstances of
the CEO's departure, there is an
opportunity to take stock of the
company's prospects and
challenges before hiring a new
CEO.   This can be very useful in
ascertaining whether an outsider
is needed and what specific

qualities the aspiring CEO must possess for a proper match with the company's needs.

Once the board has made its selection, it will have to make a formal offer, including compensation package, duration of term, performance evaluation process, circumstances and terms for termination, etc. The executive search firm, if one has been used, may be in a position to assist the board in formulating its offer. In recent times, there has been much controversy over what are perceived as excessively generous CEO compensation packages. If it is going to be an issue, the board would be wise to retain professional consultants who specialize in this sort of thing. They may have access to CEO compensation packages of comparable organizations and be in a position to advise the board. If the prospective CEO has an agent, then the board should consider retaining someone who has expertise in negotiating compensation and other terms of employment. In the end, however, both parties have to agree that a particular package is fair. The board should operate on the premise that whatever is finally agreed upon will become public knowledge at some point, and therefore can be reasonably defended.

Once hired, and at regular
intervals afterwards (usually
once a year) a CEO should
present to the board of directors
a specific plan outlining certain
objectives that he/she intends to
pursue. The board should have a
frank discussion with the CEO
about such a plan and feel free
to suggest changes. There should
be an understanding about
priorities and methodology for
the evaluation of the CEO. Where
feasible, compensation should be
linked to the performance of the
organization, provided
appropriate safeguards are in
place to prevent manipulation of
results. An increasingly common
element of performance reviews is
what is called 360 degree
evaluation. This methodology

provides for input by
subordinates and can be quite
valuable. Obviously, the
participants must be guaranteed
anonymity. As always, directors
must exercise caution in
interpreting feedback.
Circumstances can arise, for
example, where the CEO must make
unpopular, but necessary
decisions. This can skew response
by some individuals who may have
an axe to grind. No system is
perfect. Prudence and sound
judgment should always prevail.

One of the often neglected
aspects of performance evaluation
is the CEO's response to events
that could not be anticipated.
It's nice and proper that
performance be assessed on the

extent to which previously set objectives were met, but the real test of a CEO's value is how she/he deals with unexpected developments. In an ideal world, there should be contingency plans for foreseeable risks, but we do not live in an ideal world. Events outside the control or knowledge of a company or government can occur without warning. Earthquakes, tornadoes, bankruptcy of an important customer or supplier, change in government policies, labor strikes are just a few of the many factors that can suddenly have an adverse impact even on the best run enterprises.

One way in which a board can maintain an appropriate

relationship with its CEO is for
the board chair and CEO to meet
at regular intervals (monthly is
usually about right) to discuss
the major issues of the day. This
is not intended to replace the
CEO's regular reports to the
board, but to complement them.
The board chair is not the CEO's
boss and cannot give
instructions, unless the board
has given its prior approval. It
is simply an opportunity to keep
the lines of communication open.
The CEO can use the chair as a
sounding board for ideas or
problems, and the chair can
provide informal advice or
suggestions. Such a process will
contribute to a "no surprises"
environment, which is in the best
interests of all concerned.

This section would not be complete without raising the delicate issue of when and how a board should terminate its relationship with a CEO. Some cases are fairly straightforward. Fraud, deception, illegal activities, negligence, incompetence, wilful failure to disclose important information to the board are just a few of the grounds that call for termination of the employment relationship. In other cases, the individual may have done nothing wrong, but the board does not feel sufficiently confident in the CEO's ability and/or willingness to pursue certain important objectives. Perhaps the nature of the business has changed and the CEO has not kept up to date. Or,

performance may fall short of
expectations. The board should
always be alert to such
possibilities, without
jeopardizing a good working
relationship when it exists. But
if serious problems develop and
the CEO seems unable to handle
them properly, the board has a
duty to intervene. Failure to do
so places the board in a
situation where its members may
become liable for whatever damage
results from their lack of
action.

If a decision to terminate the
CEO is made by the board, several
important steps must be taken.
The first is for the board to
retain legal counsel with the
necessary expertise to advise the

board. It is important that such legal counsel be completely independent of the organization, to avoid any potential conflict of interest (real or perceived). There should be continuity of office, hence the board must name someone, generally on an interim basis, to immediately step in and take charge.

In the best case scenario, the CEO will agree to leave without making much of a fuss. The terms would be spelled out in whatever contract exists between the departing CEO and the board. If no written contract exists, then a negotiated settlement will be required. Where sufficient cause for dismissal can be legally established, there should be no

payment whatsoever. If the
company has sustained financial
losses due to the CEO's
negligence or unlawful activity,
the board has a duty to seek
compensation.

In the worst case scenario,
the CEO may not go away
willingly, or only go away upon
payment of a substantial
settlement. This is where legal
advice is necessary. A board may
want to avoid the cost and/or
publicity of a messy court battle
and agree to a monetary
settlement. Such a course of
action may be the most expedient
but not necessarily in the best
long term interests of the
company. There are no firm rules
that can always be applied to

such situations. As I have indicated before, the value of a board of directors lies in the judgment calls that it makes.

This brings me to the last point that I would like to make. And that is the board's duty to evaluate its own performance. There are many questionnaires, designed for different types of boards, that can be used by a board to evaluate how effectively it is discharging its responsibilities. They often include a 360 degree participation element, as described earlier. The object of any such exercise is to improve performance and to ensure that the board remains focussed on important, rather than routine matters. Not everybody is comfortable with this type of process. It is not something that can be imposed on a board. Each director must feel that it is worthwhile. When properly done, however, it can produce valuable results that will improve the effectiveness of a board's governance.

NOTE TO READERS

If you found this manual useful, please consider advising your contacts who may be interested.

Print copies may be purchased from: www.createspace.com. E-book copies are available from www.amazon.com.

Feedback may be sent to me through my website: www.cbc-manera.com.

Tony Manera